Bill Clinton

WILLIAM JEFFERSON CLINTON
(1946–   )

QUOTATIONS

OF

William Jefferson Clinton

APPLEWOOD BOOKS
Carlisle, Massachusetts

ISBN 978-1-55709-065-2

10 9 8 7 6 5 4 3 2

MANUFACTURED IN THE UNITED STATES OF AMERICA
WITH AMERICAN-MADE MATERIALS

William Jefferson Clinton

PRESIDENT CLINTON was born William Jefferson
Blythe III on August 19, 1946, in Hope, Arkansas,
three months after his father died in a traffic
accident. When he was four years old, his mother
wed Roger Clinton of Hot Springs, Arkansas.
In high school, he took the family name.

He excelled as a student and as a saxophone
player and once considered becoming a musician.
As a delegate to Boys Nation while in high
school, he met President John Kennedy at the
White House. The encounter led him to enter
a life of public service.

Clinton graduated from Georgetown University
and in 1968 won a Rhodes Scholarship to Oxford
University. He received a law degree from Yale
University in 1973 and entered politics in Arkansas.

He was defeated in his campaign for Congress
in Arkansas's Third District in 1974. The next
year he married Hillary Rodham, a graduate of
Wellesley College and Yale Law School. In 1980,
Chelsea, their only child, was born.

Clinton was elected Arkansas attorney
general in 1976 and won the governorship in
1978. After losing a bid for a second term, he
regained the office four years later, and served
until he defeated incumbent George Bush and
third-party candidate Ross Perot in the 1992
presidential race.

Clinton and his running mate, Tennessee senator Albert Gore Jr., then forty-four, represented a new generation in American political leadership. And for the first time in twelve years both the White House and Congress were held by the same party. But that political edge was brief: the Republicans won both houses of Congress in 1994.

As president, Clinton successfully dispatched peacekeeping forces to war-torn Bosnia and ordered the bombing of Iraq when Saddam Hussein stopped United Nations inspections for evidence of nuclear, chemical, and biological weapons. He became a global proponent for an expanded NATO, more-open international trade, and a worldwide campaign against drug trafficking. He drew huge crowds when he traveled, advocating U.S.-style freedom.

In 1998, Clinton became the second U.S. president to be impeached by the House of Representatives. He was tried in the Senate and found not guilty of the charges brought against him. He remained a very popular president.

After leaving office in 2001, he established the William J. Clinton Foundation, with the mission "to improve global health, strengthen economies, promote healthier childhoods, and protect the environment by fostering partnerships among governments, businesses, nongovernmental organizations, and private citizens to turn good intentions into measurable results."

QUOTATIONS
OF
William Jefferson
Clinton

*I*t is time to heal America. And so we must say to every American: Look beyond the stereotypes that blind us. We need each other. All of us—we need each other. We don't have a person to waste.

Democratic Convention Acceptance Speech, 1992

Bill Clinton

*I*f you live long enough, you'll make mistakes. But if you learn from them, you'll be a better person. It's how you handle adversity, not how it affects you. The main thing is never quit, never quit, never quit.

Campaign Speech, June 1992

I ask you to join in a re-United States. We need to empower our people so they can take more responsibility for their own lives in a world that is ever smaller, where everyone counts.

Speech to Supporters in Little Rock, Arkansas, November 4, 1992

Bill Clinton

*O*ur democracy must be not only the envy of the world but the engine of our own renewal. There is nothing wrong with America that cannot be cured by what is right with America.

First Inaugural Address, January 20, 1993

Bill Clinton

*E*ach generation of Americans must define what it means to be an American.

First Inaugural Address, January 20, 1993

Our Founders saw themselves in the light
of posterity. We can do no less. Anyone who
has ever watched a child's eyes wander into
sleep knows what posterity is. Posterity is
the world to come—the world for whom
we hold our ideals, from whom we have
borrowed our planet, and to whom we
bear sacred responsibility.

First Inaugural Address, January 20, 1993

Bill Clinton

Though our challenges are fearsome, so
are our strengths. And Americans have ever
been a restless, questing, hopeful people. We
must bring to our task today the vision and
will of those who came before us.

First Inaugural Address, January 20, 1993

*T*hough we march to the music of our time, our mission is timeless.

> *First Inaugural Address, January 20, 1993*

Bill Clinton

*P*rofound and powerful forces are shaking and remaking our world. And the urgent question of our time is whether we can make change our friend and not our enemy.

> *First Inaugural Address, January 20, 1993*

Bill Clinton

*T*he price of doing the same old thing is far higher than the price of change.

> *Presidents' Day, February 1993*

We honor these valiant men and women not for dying, because death comes to all of us eventually. We honor them for how they died and how they lived. In life, they gave us aid when we were helpless, shielded us when we were vulnerable, lifted us when we had fallen, gave us comfort when we were afraid. In rooting out our lawless, they preserved our order. They were our fathers and sons, our brothers and sisters, our mothers and daughters. They were our friends. Their contributions cannot be measured nor properly honored by their President or any other citizen, except to say a single thank you and give a prayer to God for their souls. They will be remembered, as all of you knew them, standing tall and ready, the sentinels of our Liberty. Let us live in ways that will honor their ultimate contribution to our lives.

Remarks at the National Law Enforcement Officers Memorial Ceremony, May 13, 1993

*J*ust as war is freedom's cost, disagreement
is freedom's privilege.

> *Ceremony at the Vietnam Veterans*
> *Memorial, May 31, 1993*

Bill Clinton

*L*et us learn here once again the simple,
powerful, beautiful lesson, the simple faith
of Robert Kennedy: We can do better. Let us
leave here no longer in two places, but once
again in one only: in the here and now, with
a commitment to tomorrow, the only part
of our time that we can control.

> *25th Anniversary Memorial Mass for*
> *Robert F. Kennedy, June 6, 1993*

We Americans are a people both privileged and challenged. We were formed in turbulent times, and we stand now at the beginning of a new time, the dawn of a new era. Our deeds and decisions can lift America up so that in our third century we will continue to be the youngest and most optimistic of nations, a people on the march once again, strong and unafraid. If we are bold in our hopes, if we meet our great responsibilities, we will give the country we love the best years it has ever known.

*Address to the Nation on the
Economic Program, August 3, 1993*

Bill Clinton

What we can do in Washington is in no small measure determined by what lives in the hearts and minds and visions of Americans throughout this land.

*Remarks to the National Urban League,
August 4, 1993*

Yesterday is yesterday. If we try to recapture it, we will only lose tomorrow.

Speech at University of North Carolina, October 1993

Bill Clinton

I do not believe we can repair the basic fabric of society until people who are willing to work have work. Work organizes life. It gives structure and discipline to life.

86th Annual Holy Convocation, Church of God in Christ, Memphis, Tennessee, November 13, 1993

Bill Clinton

The future is not an inheritance. It is an opportunity and an obligation.

Remarks to UCLA 75th Anniversary Convocation, May 20, 1994

*A*voiding today's problems would be our own generation's appeasements. For just as freedom has a price, it also has a purpose, and its name is progress.

> U.S. National Cemetery,
> D-day Ceremonies, June 6, 1994

Bill Clinton

*T*he work of freedom is not easy. It requires discipline, responsibility, and a faith strong enough to endure failure and criticism. And it requires vigilance

> Remarks at the Brandenburg Gate, June 12, 1994

Bill Clinton

*B*eing president is like running a cemetery: you've got a lot of people under you and nobody's listening.

> Remarks at Carl Sandburg Community College,
> Galesburg, Illinois, January 10, 1995

*T*he road to tyranny, we must never forget,
begins with the destruction of the truth.

*Dedication of the Thomas J. Dodd Research Center,
Storrs, Connecticut, October 15, 1995*

Bill Clinton

*N*o good house was ever built on a bad
foundation. Nothing good ever came of hate.

Address on Race Relations, October 16, 1995

Bill Clinton

*Y*our destiny is for you to determine. Only
you can decide between division and unity,
between hard lives and high hopes. Only
you can create a lasting peace. It takes
courage to let go of familiar divisions.
It takes faith to walk down a new road.

*Address to the Employees of the Mackie Metal Plant,
Northern Ireland, November 30, 1995*

When I took office, only high-energy
physicists had ever heard of what is called
the Worldwide Web.... Now even my cat
has its own page.

*Announcement of the Next Generation
Internet Initiative, 1996*

Bill Clinton

You need to know that a member of
Congress who refuses to allow the minimum
wage to come up for a vote made more
money during last year's one-month
government shutdown than a minimum
wage worker makes in an entire year.

Weekly Radio Address, March 31, 1996

I have always believed that the decision
to have an abortion generally should
be between a woman, her doctor, her
conscience, and her God.

Veto Message, H.R. 1833, April 10, 1996

Bill Clinton

Where our children are concerned, we
should all stand together, and we should not
be small. Our children are counting on us.

Radio Address, June 1, 1996

Bill Clinton

You can put wings on a pig, but you don't
make it an eagle.

Speech at Sacramento, California, July 23, 1996

We can only build our bridge to the 21st century if we build it together, and if we're willing to walk arm in arm across that bridge together.

*Speech at Democratic National Convention,
Chicago, August 29, 1996*

Bill Clinton

I still believe in a place called Hope, a place called America.

*Speech at Democratic National Convention,
Chicago, August 29, 1996*

Bill Clinton

We must keep our old Democracy forever young. Guided by the ancient vision of a Promised Land. Let us set our sights upon a land of new promise.

Second Inaugural Address, January 20, 1997

*A*merica demands and deserves big things from us, and nothing big ever came from being small.

Second Inaugural Address, January 20, 1997

Bill Clinton

*O*ur rich texture of racial, religious and political diversity will be a Godsend in the 21st century. Great rewards will come to those who can live together, learn together, work together, forge new ties that bind together.

Second Inaugural Address, January 20, 1997

*T*he greatest progress we have made, and the greatest progress we have yet to make, is in the human heart. In the end, all the world's wealth and a thousand armies are no match for the strength and decency of the human spirit.

Second Inaugural Address, January 20, 1997

Bill Clinton

*T*he real differences around the world today are not between Jews and Arabs; Protestants and Catholics; Muslims, Croats, and Serbs. The real differences are between those who embrace peace and those who would destroy it; between those who look to the future and those who cling to the past; between those who open their arms and those who are determined to clench their fists.

Speech to U.S. Troops in Bosnia, December 22, 1997

*L*ight still shines amid the dark places
of our world. It is reflected in the lives of
so many quiet and generous people who
strive daily to make life better for others—
feeding the hungry, caring for the ill and
elderly, cherishing and nurturing children. It
radiates from the hearts of those who work
for peace and justice in their communities,
our nation, and the world. It shines in the
efforts of men and women striving to break
down the walls of fear, ignorance, and
prejudice that cast shadows across too many
lives and prevent us from becoming the
people God intended us to be.

Message on the Observance of Christmas,
December 22, 1997

We do know that we must do more to reach out to our children and teach them to express their anger and to resolve their conflicts with words, not weapons.

Nationally Televised News Conference on the Columbine High School Shootings, April 21, 1999

Bill Clinton

When our memories outweigh our dreams, we have grown old.

Remarks at America's Millennium Gala, Lincoln Memorial, December 31, 1999

Bill Clinton

When we make college more affordable, we make the American dream more achievable.

Remarks at College Affordability Event, White House, January 20, 2000

We should, all of us, be filled with gratitude and humility for our present progress and prosperity. We should be filled with awe and joy at what lies over the horizon. And we should be filled with absolute determination to make the most of it.

State of the Union Address, January 27, 2000

Bill Clinton

We cannot build our own future without helping others to build theirs.

State of the Union Address, January 27, 2000

$\mathcal{B}$ecause we want to live in a world which is not dominated by a division of people who live on the cutting edge of a new economy and others who live on the bare edge of survival, we must be involved.

Clinton Remarks at Opening of National Summit on Africa, White House, February 17, 2000

Bill Clinton

In the new economy, information, education, and motivation are everything.

Remarks to the Joint Session of the Indian Parliament, New Delhi, March 22, 2000

When Galileo discovered he could use
the tools of mathematics and mechanics to
understand the motion of celestial bodies, he
felt, in the words of one eminent researcher,
that he had learned the language in which
God recreated the universe. Today we are
learning the language in which God created
life. We are gaining ever more awe for the
complexity, the beauty, the wonder
of God's most divine and sacred gift.

*From White House Press Conference
on the publication of the First Draft of
the Human Genome, June 26, 2000*

Bill Clinton

Today, many companies are reporting
that their number one constraint on growth
is the inability to hire workers with the
necessary skills.

*Statement on Signing the American Competitiveness
in the Twenty-First Century Act, October 17, 2000*

*B*y lifting the weakest, poorest among us,
we lift the rest of us as well.

Debt Relief Bill Signing, November 6, 2000

Bill Clinton

*G*olf is like life in a lot of ways—all the
biggest wounds are self-inflicted.

Interview in Golf Digest, November 2000

Bill Clinton

*P*eace is not a spectator sport....
The enemies of peace don't need your
approval. All they need is your apathy.

Speech in Northern Ireland, December 2000

Globalization is not something we can hold off or turn off...it is the economic equivalent of a force of nature—like wind or water.

Speech at Vietnam National University in Hanoi, November 17, 2000

Bill Clinton

Global poverty is a powder keg that could be ignited by our indifference.

Farewell Address, January 18, 2001

Bill Clinton

As we become ever more diverse, we must work harder to unite around our common values and our common humanity.

Farewell Address, January 18, 2001

A world without walls is the only sustainable world.... If the world is dominated by people who believe that their races, their religions, their ethnic differences are the most important factors, then a huge number of people will perish in this century.

Speech at Zellerbach Hall, U.C.-Berkeley,
January 29, 2002

*P*olitics is not religion and we should govern on the basis of evidence, not theology.

Booksellers Convention in Chicago, June 2004

*S*trength and wisdom are not opposing values.

Democratic National Convention, July 26, 2004

*A*merica just works better when more people have a chance to live their dreams.

Democratic National Convention, July 26, 2004

Bill Clinton

*W*hat should our shared values be? Everybody counts. Everybody deserves a chance. Everybody's got a responsibility to fulfill.

Unveiling of the Clinton Presidential Library, November 18, 2004

*B*uilding bridges...we have to spend
our lives building a global community
and an American community of shared
responsibilities, shared values, shared
benefits. [This library] is the symbol of not
only what I tried to do, but what I want to
do, with the rest of my life. Building bridges
from yesterday to tomorrow. Building bridges
across racial and religion and ethnic and
income and political divides.

Unveiling of the Clinton Presidential Library,
November 18, 2004

Bill Clinton

*Y*ou don't have to wait till your party's in
power to have an impact on life at home and
around the world.

Speech at Campus Progress National
Student Conference, July 13, 2005

I think the best social program is a job.

> *Annual Dinner of the Economic Club*
> *of Grand Rapids, June 18, 2007*

Bill Clinton

*W*hen we give what we can and give it
with joy, we don't just renew the American
tradition of giving, we also renew ourselves.

> *Woman's Day, July 10, 2007*

Bill Clinton

*I*n the years ahead, I will never hold a
position higher or a covenant more sacred
than that of President of the United States.
But there is no title I will wear more proudly
than that of citizen.

> *Farewell Address, January 18, 2001*

Bill Clinton